HISTORY & GEOGRAPHY 208
MESSAGES FROM NEAR AND FAR

CONTENTS

Author: **Barbara Smith**
Editor: Richard W Wheeler, M.A.Ed.
Consulting Editor: Howard Stitt, Th.M., Ed.D.
Revision Editor: Alan Christopherson, M.S.

Alpha Omega Publications®

804 N. 2nd Ave. E., Rock Rapids, IA 51246-1759

Learn with our friends:

When you see me, I will help your teacher explain the exciting things you are expected to do.

When you do actions with me, you will learn how to write, draw, match words, read, and much more.

You and I will learn about matching words, listening, drawing, and other fun things in your lessons.

MESSAGES FROM NEAR AND FAR

Communication is the way in which people talk to one another. You can communicate in many ways. In this LIFEPAC® you will learn about communication in Bible times. You will learn how communication has gotten bigger and faster today. You will also find out why everyone needs communication. Best of all, you will learn more about communication with God, your heavenly Father.

Objectives

Read these objectives. They tell you what you will be able to do when you have finished this LIFEPAC.

1. You will be able to tell how people communicated in Bible times.

2. You will be able to tell many ways to communicate today.

3. You will be able to talk about why communication is important to everyone.

4. You will be able to tell how to communicate without making a sound.

camera (cam er a). A machine used to take pictures.

communication (com mun i ca tion). The way people talk to each other.

computer (com pu ter). A machine that can do mathematics and other things quickly.

crowds. A lot of people.

diary (di a ry). A daily record of events.

expression (ex pres sion). A look on a face showing the feelings of the person.

important (im por tant). Something that means a lot.

message (mes sage). Communication by writing or talking.

mime. Using only movements to show a story.

newspaper (news pa per). A paper you can buy that tells you what is happening in the world.

papyrus (pa py rus). A writing material, like paper, made from plants.

parchment (parch ment). Skin of sheep or goat used for writing.

printing press (print ing press). Machine for making a lot of copies of written things.

problem (prob lem). Something wrong that needs to be fixed.

satellite (sat el lite). A machine that circles the earth and helps send messages and signals.

scribe. A person whose job is writing for other people.

scroll. Papyrus or parchment rolled on two sticks for writing a message.

signal (sig nal). To communicate by sound or action.

tablets (ta b lets). Flat pieces of stone used for writing .

telegraph (tel e graph). A way to send a message over wires.

telephone (phone) (tel e phone). A way to talk to someone far away.

television (tel e vi sion). An invention that sends pictures and sound through the air.

translator (trans la tor). A person who can help two people with different languages to understand each other.

 These words will appear in **boldface** (darker print) the first time they are used.

I. COMMUNICATION IN BIBLE TIMES

In Bible times people **communicated** mostly by talking to each other. Some things were put in writing but many of the people living then could not read or write. The people could understand each other through pictures or hand and face **messages**, too. A nod of the head or a hand wave would have been as good as many words, just as they are now.

Ask your teacher to say these words with you.

WORDS TO STUDY

communication (com mu ni ca tion) The way that people talk to each other.

message (mes sage) Communication by writing or talking.

papyrus (pa py rus) A writing material, like paper, made from plants.

parchment (parch ment) Skin of sheep or goat used for writing.

scribe A person whose job is writing for other people.

scroll Papyrus or parchment rolled on two sticks for writing a message.

tablets (tab lets) Flat pieces of stone used for writing.

Ask your teacher to say these words with you.

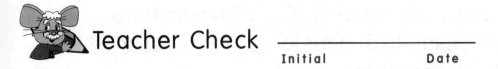

Teacher Check _____
　　　　　　　　Initial　　　　　　Date

TALKING AND LISTENING

Communication always needs at least two people. When God made Adam, the first man, Adam was lonely. He had a garden and a lot of animals, but Adam had no one to talk to. God made Eve as a companion for Adam. Now Adam and Eve could talk to each other. Each night God would come and talk to them, too. But Adam and Eve did not always listen to God. They did not obey Him. God told them not to eat the fruit from one tree. They ate it anyway. God had to send them out of their garden. God could not come and talk to them. Now Adam and Eve did not talk about happy things all the time, but they were still friends.

When Jesus was on earth, He talked to a lot of people. The people He talked to most were His friends, the disciples. They listened to Him and believed what He said. The disciples tried to do what Jesus told them to do. Jesus talked to **crowds** of people, too. Many of them believed what Jesus said and followed Him. But many did not like what Jesus said. These people killed Jesus, but He came back to life.

People now can communicate with God through Jesus. They talk to the heavenly Father just as they talk to their father on earth.

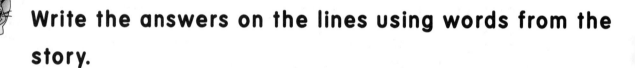

Write the answers on the lines using words from the story.

1.1   Communication needs _____ people.

1.2   Adam was lonely, so God made _____ .

1.3   Now Adam talked to _____ and to _____ .

1.4   Adam and Eve did not _____ and obey.

1.5   God could not come and _____ to them.

1.6   Jesus talked mostly to His _____ .

1.7   Jesus also talked to _____ of

       people.

1.8   Many people listened and _____

       what Jesus said.

1.9   People who did not like what Jesus said decided to

       _____ Him.

WRITING AND SENDING MESSAGES

Tablets for the Ten Commandments

Long before Jesus was on earth, God had a very important **message** He wanted to give to His people. God wanted the people to remember what He said. So God wrote His message down. He wrote it on large flat pieces of stone called **tablets**. What God wrote were rules for His people to follow. They were called the Ten Commandments. Moses, the leader of God's people, went up on a mountain. Moses brought down the tablets with the Ten Commandments. He read them to the people.

Later, when Jesus was on earth, parts of the Bible were written down on papyrus. Papyrus was like paper but was made from a papyrus plant, a reed plant, found near the water. The papyrus was made into pulp and dried into long sheets

Scroll

and rolled on two sticks. The people called it a **scroll**. Men wrote on scrolls. Books of bound paper were unknown then. Men who could write got jobs as **scribes**. A scribe would write down what someone else wanted written or would copy another scroll so that several people could have the same writing. Later these scrolls were made from parchment. **Parchment** was a writing material made from dried and scraped animal skins.

When Jesus read God's Word, He read from a scroll. Paul's letters to the churches were written on scrolls.

Draw lines to match.

1.10	papyrus	flat pieces of stone
1.11	scribes	went to get the Ten Commandments
1.12	tablets	like paper for writing
1.13	Ten Commandments	got jobs writing
1.14	scroll	God's rules for His people
1.15	parchment	wrote letters to churches
1.16	Moses	books rolled on two sticks
1.17	Paul	made from animal skins

Do this activity.

1.18   You can make a scroll if you follow the steps. The pictures will help.

     1.   Take a piece of drawing paper.

     2.   Cut it in half the long way.

     3.   Glue the two pieces together so you can have one long piece.

     4.   On each end glue a popsicle stick or some used pencils.

     5.   Write your favorite Bible verse on the paper.

     6.   Roll up your scroll from both ends.

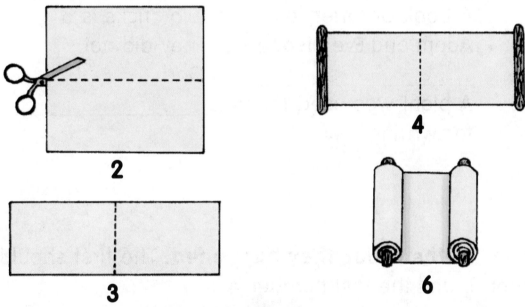

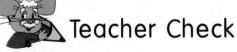

Steps for Making Scroll

Show your teacher your finished scroll.

Teacher Check _____

             Initial   Date

Review
REVIEW
Review

      For this Self Test, study what you have read and done. The Self Test will check what you remember.

SELF TEST 1

Write these words in the right blanks.

parchment   communication
papyrus   scroll
disciples   listen

1.01   Something made from animal skins and used to write on was _____ .

1.02   The people Jesus talked to the most were His

_____ .

1.03   Two people are needed to have _____ .

1.04   A book or letter rolled on two sticks is a _____ .

1.05   Adam and Eve disobeyed. They did not
_____ to God.

1.06   A plant was used to make _____
for writing.

Number in the order they happened. The first should be number 1 and the last number 4.

1.07   _____ talking

1.08   _____ Ten Commandments

1.09   _____ parchment

1.010   _____ papyrus

Answer these questions.

1.011 Why did God make Eve? _____

_____

1.012 What were the Ten Commandments? _____

_____

_____

EACH ANSWER, 1 POINT

 Teacher Check _____

Initial   Date

My Score

II. COMMUNICATION IN MODERN TIMES

Since Bible times men have thought of
new ways to communicate with each
other. They have learned to talk over
long distances. Writing is no longer done
only by hand. Pictures and sounds can be
sent over air waves and even to and from
space.

WORDS TO STUDY

computer   (com pu ter)   A machine that can do mathematics and other things quickly.

important   (im por tant)   Something that means a lot.

newspaper   (news pa per)   A paper you can buy that tells you what is happening in the world.

printing press   (print ing press)   Machine for making a lot of copies of written things.

satellite   (sat el lite)   A machine that circles the earth and helps send messages and signals.

signal   (sig nal)   To communicate by sound or action.

telegraph   (tel e graph)   A way to send a message over wires.

telephone (phone)   (tel e phone)   A way to talk to someone far away.

television   (tel e vi sion)   An invention that sends pictures and sound through the air.

Ask your teacher to say these words with you.

Teacher Check _____

WRITING

The work of making parchment and writing it by hand made a book very hard to get in days gone by. What a big step forward it was when paper and print were made. First paper was made from cloth. Today most paper is made of wood pulp. But the most **important** invention was the **printing press**. The printing press had movable pieces of print that could be set up as a page for a book. With ink rolled over the print and paper pressed onto it, a whole page was made at one time. Many pages could be made easily before the next page of print was set up. The writing did not have to be done by hand each time. After a long time, books became common and did not cost so much.

The first book printed was the Bible. Today, huge presses make **newspapers** every day. Just about everyone can read the news and know what is happening in the world.

Being able to send messages by mail is another big step in communication. A person can write a letter, put a stamp on it, and send it anywhere in the world. At first letters were carried by horses and riders. This way was called the Pony Express. Today most mail travels by airplane and truck.

Answer these questions by looking in your story.

2.1   What was paper first made of?

_____

2.2   What is most paper made from today?

_____

2.3   What paper tells people what is happening in the world?

_____

2.4   What was the most important invention?

_____

2.5   What did they call it when horses and riders carried the mail?

_____

2.6   How do most letters travel today?

_____

TALKING AND TELEPHONES

People still talk to other people. As man found out more about his world, he used what he learned to communicate from distances.

Over 100 years ago the **telegraph** was invented. The telegraph was a way of sending messages over wires. Samuel Morse made up an alphabet of dots and dashes known as the Morse Code. These long and short signals were sent great distances over wires.

The next step was made by Alexander Graham Bell. He believed voices could be sent along a wire, too. After a lot of thought and work, Bell invented the **telephone**. Today we can talk to someone hundreds of miles away using a phone.

Write the lines using words from the story.

2.7   The man who invented the telephone was

_____ .

2.8   The man who made the alphabet of dots and dashes

was _____ .

2.9   These dots and dashes are called the _____

_____ .

2.10   Sending coded messages over wires uses the

_____ .

2.11   People can still _____ from a

distance.

Just for fun:

2.12   Here is the Morse Code. Write a word or sentence in

code. Have a friend figure it out. Be sure to leave large

spaces between each letter and word.

A	• —	N	— •
B	— • • •	O	— — —
C	— • — •	P	• — — •
D	— • •	Q	— — • —
E	•	R	• — •
F	• • — •	S	• • •
G	— — •	T	—
H	• • • •	U	• • —
I	• •	V	• • • —
J	• — — —	W	• — —
K	— • —	X	— • • —
L	• — • •	Y	— • — —
M	— —	Z	— — • •

RADIO AND TELEVISION TO COMPUTERS AND CELL PHONES

The time came when men decided that sound could be sent without wires. They learned that voices and music could be sent through the air and picked up by a special receiver. This invention was first called the wireless. After a while it became the radio. People used the radio for listening to music, stories and the news. Radio, digital media players, **computers**, and cell phones are used in the same way today.

The next invention sent pictures through the air. The receiver for the pictures was the **television**. The first television was in black and white. Now we have color televisions, computers, and cell phones. The Olympic Games can be seen from a faraway country and the president can be seen and heard on any of these devices.

 Circle yes if the sentence is true. Circle no if the sentence is not true.

2.13   Sound can be sent without wires.   yes   no

2.14   The wireless is what we call

Morse Code.   yes   no

2.15   Man can send pictures through
        the air.   yes   no

2.16   We can hear the news on the
        radio.   yes   no

2.17   The first pictures sent through the
        air were in color.   yes   no

2.18   You can see the person you are
        talking to on some cell phones.   yes   no

SATELLITES AND COMPUTERS

To make pictures travel farther, **satellites** are used. Satellites travel in space around the earth. They pick up **signals** and send them out again. This way a television station on one side of the world can send a signal to a satellite. The satellite sends the signal on to a station on the other side of the world. One famous satellite is named Telstar.

Computers are a very important way to communicate. At first computers were just machines that could do mathematics very fast. Now they do much more. They store

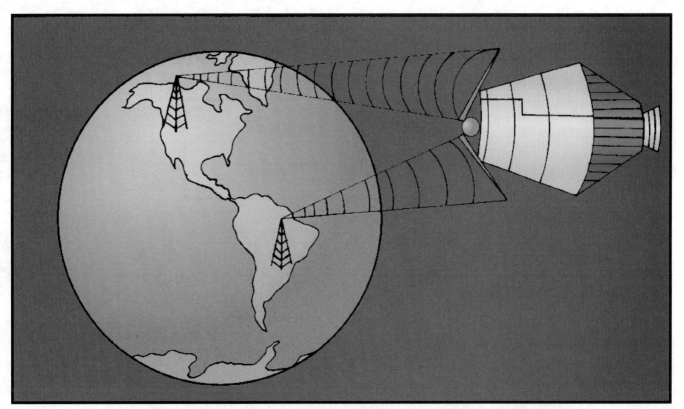

Satellite Sending and Receiving Signals

words and thoughts and sort through them for particular things. Stores now use computers to check groceries out and to reorder them at the same time. Computers can solve hard problems quickly. Computers are used by airlines to help make sure you get on the right plane. Computers are now used in business and science.

Tell whether it is talking about a satellite or a computer by putting 1 or 2 on the line.

1. satellite
2. computer

2.19 _____ Telstar

2.20 _____ machines to do fast mathematics

2.21 _____ travel around the earth

2.22 _____ send television signals around the world

2.23 _____ solve problems fast

2.24 _____ can save words and thoughts

2.25 _____ picks up signals and sends them out again

2.26 _____ can help you get on the right plane

Do these activities about the long /ē/ sound.

2.27 The long /ē/ sound is spelled more than one way. Write in the blanks the letters at the beginning of each row. These letters are different ways to spell long ē.

a. EA   M ____ ____ T   R ____ ____ D

b. EE   S ____ ____ D   F ____ ____ L

c. IE   P ____ ____ CE   BEL ____ ____ VE

d. EI   REC ____ ____ VE

e. E   B ____   TH ____ SE

2.28   Write one more word for each long ē spelling.

      a. EA _____   IE _____   E _____
      b. EE _____   EI _____

Teacher Check _____
                  Initial   Date

Study what you have read and done for this Self Test. This Self Test will check what you remember of this part and other parts you have read.

SELF TEST 2

Write the right answer on the lines.

2.01   Many copies of a piece of writing could be made on a

    _____ .

    printing press   paper   telephone

2.02   Most paper today is made of _____ .

    cloth   wood   sand

2.03   An early way to send mail was called the

    _____ .

    Pony Express   Parcel Post   Airmail

2.04   The man who invented the telephone was

    _____ .

    Alexander G. Bell   Samuel Morse   Abe Lincoln

2.05 Using dots and dashes to send messages is called

_____.

    telegraph   Morse Code   satellite

2.06 A book rolled on two sticks is a _____.

    parchment   scroll   newspaper

2.07 A radio used to be called a _____.

    wireless   telephone   telegraph

2.08 Something that helps send signals around the world

is a _____.

    computer   satellite   credit card

Circle yes if the sentence is true. Circle no if the sentence is not true.

2.09	You can send sound without wires.	yes	no
2.010	Communication needs at least two people.	yes	no
2.011	Large flat pieces of stone are called parchment.	yes	no
2.012	The Ten Commandments were God's rules.	yes	no
2.013	Newspapers tell people what is happening in the world.	yes	no
2.014	Computers are machines that can do mathematics fast.	yes	no

EACH ANSWER, 1 POINT

11 / 14

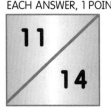

 Teacher Check _____

                    Initial   Date

 My Score

HISTORY & GEOGRAPHY

2 0 8

LIFEPAC TEST

14 / 18

Name _____

Date _____

Score _____

HISTORY AND GEOGRAPHY 208: LIFEPAC TEST

EACH ANSWER, 1 POINT

Write the right answer on each line.

1. The thing that carries pictures around the world is a
    _____ .

    translator   satellite

2. The thing that made it possible to make many copies of
    writing very fast was the _____ .

    printing press   wireless

3. The radio used to be called the _____ .

    wireless   telephone

4. A person who helps two people that speak different
    languages to communicate is a _____ .

    telegraph   translator

5. Radios send _____ into the air.

    computers   signals

6. People _____ if they want to
    understand what others say.

    listen   mime

7. A set of dots and dashes used to send telegraph
    messages is _____ .

    Morse Code   Bell Code

Write yes **if the sentence is true. Write** no **if the sentence is not true.**

8. _____ Communication can help countries work together.

9. _____ Jesus talked and many people believed what He said.

10. _____ The first paper was made from mud.

11. _____ A printing press can make many copies of writing.

12. _____ Most jobs use talking to communicate.

13. _____ People today send messages by horseback.

Answer these questions.

14. What are two things you can do to show your pleasure to someone without talking? a. _____
    b. _____ .

15. What does it take to have communication?

    _____

16. Why did God make Eve? _____

17. What are the Ten Commandments? _____

NOTES

III. COMMUNICATION FOR EVERYONE

Imagine someone all alone on a desert island. They would have no phone or radio. They would have no pets. They would have no one to talk to. They would be very lonely. Remember that God gave Adam a wife, Eve. God gave Adam a wife so he would have someone to talk to. Everyone needs to be able to communicate. Sometimes it is hard to say the right things. This section will help you see why communication is so important.

WORDS TO STUDY

camera   (cam er a)   A machine used to take pictures.

problem   (prob lem)   Something wrong that needs to be fixed.

translator (trans la tor)   A person who can help two people with different languages to understand each other.

Ask your teacher to say these words with you

FAMILIES

God thought families were important. He made Adam and Eve and told them to have children. To have a happy family, mother, father, and children need to talk to each other. Parents need to tell their children that they love them. They need to let their children know the rules to follow. They need to teach them. Children need to talk with their family, too. Families are their own best friends. Children should ask their parents when they have questions. They should tell them when they are afraid of things. They need to let them know how they feel. Life is happier if people explain and listen and try to understand each other.

Brothers and sisters are fun to talk with, too. They can be helpful and playful. Even when someone in the family goes away, they can still communicate. They can write letters or talk on the phone. Without communication it is very hard to have a happy family.

Answer each question with yes **or** no.

3.1 God thought families were important.

_____

3.2 Communication is not very important to a family.

_____

3.3 Your dog is your best friend.

_____

3.4 You should tell your parents how you feel.

_____

3.5 When someone goes away you cannot communicate anymore.

_____

3.6 Without communication it is very hard to have a happy family.

_____

Do this activity.

3.7 Think of one nice thing to say to each person in your family. Go home tonight and say it to them. Tomorrow answer these questions.

a. How do you think your words made your family feel?

_____

b. How did it make you feel? _____

_____

_____

JOBS

Think about all the different kinds of jobs people have to do. Most of them would be very hard to do without some communication. Nearly all jobs need talking. Some jobs use other kinds of communication as well.

A teacher talks and listens and writes. A teacher uses books, pictures, CDs, and DVDs to help children learn.

A doctor needs to be able to listen to his patient and then to explain the problem. He and his nurse must know the names of special tools and pills.

A taxi driver uses a radio to find out where he is supposed to go. Telephone workers, policemen, and street workers also have radios in their cars for talking and listening.

A fireman uses a phone to answer fire alarms. He uses radios to tell the firemen where to go. He also uses a loudspeaker to make sure everyone can hear directions during the fire fighting. Afterwards the fireman has to write a report that tells about the fire.

All these new ways of communication have made new jobs, too. Today we need people to tell us the news. People are needed to run the television cameras. Many jobs are open for people who know how to fix all the new machines if they break. The world of work uses communication!

Do this activity.

3.8   Here are some kinds of communication. Put the right numbers after each job to tell what kind of communication the jobs use. Some will have more than one kind. Use your story to remind you of the kinds of communication each job uses.

1. Special words
2. Books
3. Radios
4. Phone

5. Talking
6. Loudspeaker
7. Writing

a. Teacher   _____

b. Doctor   _____

c. Policeman   _____

d. Taxi driver   _____

e. Fireman   _____

Answer this question.

3.9   What are two jobs made by having these new ways of communicating?

a. _____

b. _____

Do this reading activity.

Beginning g with j sound; beginning c with s sound

3.10   Here is a silly story using words beginning with a g that sounds like j and with a c that sounds like s. Write in the words so that the story makes sense. Use each word only once. The first letter of each word has been filled in for you.

ceiling   giant

circus   giraffe

city   George

circle   germ

     One day a big tent with lots of animals came to our

c _____ . We knew it was a

c_____ when we saw the

clowns. But one clown looked sad. He couldn't find the

tall g_____ whose name was

G_____ . He looked everywhere. Finally

he looked in the tent. There was George. He was

nearly as tall as a g_____ .

He was standing in the round c_____ .

He was looking way up at the c_____ .

page 28 (twenty-eight)

"What are you doing?" asked the clown. "Just watching a g_____ eat the tent," he answered calmly!

3.11   Now read the story to your teacher.

Teacher Check _____
                Initial   Date

COUNTRIES

The leaders of different countries need to communicate. If the world is to remain peaceful, the leaders need to talk about **problems**. Talking can help different countries to get along better with each other. Sometimes it can help stop wars. The leaders also talk about ways to help each other. Some countries do not have enough food. Some countries do not have enough gas. Some need help building special machines. Communication can help countries work together.

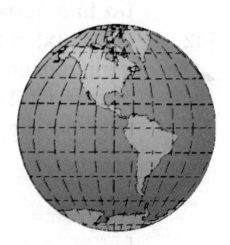

Different Countries

Sometimes countries have a hard time communicating. Countries have different ways of doing things. Many countries have different languages. The leaders use someone special to help them communicate. This person is called a **translator.** A translator can speak two or more languages. He can tell the leaders what each one is saying. He talks to them in their own language. Communication does not always work. Sometimes communication between countries helps make the world a little better for everyone to live in.

Do this activity.

3.12 Put an **(x)** in front of each group of words that is a good reason for countries to communicate. Do not put anything if it is not a good reason for communication. Use your story to help you.

a. _____ Helps stop wars

b. _____ Talks about problems

c. _____ Helps get more food

d. _____ Makes people angry

e. _____ Helps build special machines

f. _____ Starts wars

g. _____ Helps make the world better to live in

Write the answers on the lines.

3.13   A person who helps people with different languages to communicate is a _____ .

3.14   A translator can talk in _____ languages.

3.15   A translator talks to each person in his own _____

_____ .

Do this activity about the long / ī / sound.

3.16   The long / ī / sound is spelled more than one way.

      1. -i like in kite

      2. -igh like in night

      3. -y like in sky

Put the number (1, 2, or 3) that tells which spelling of the long / ī / sound each word uses.

3.17   a. _____ light   g. _____ sight

      b. _____ try   h. _____ high

      c. _____ lion   i. _____ why

      d. _____ climb   j. _____ bright

      e. _____ good-bye   k. _____ fine

      f. _____ like   l. _____ cry

Review REVIEW Review   Study what you have read and done for this Self Test. This Self Test will check what you remember of this part and other parts you have read.

SELF TEST 3

Check (✓) the best ending to each sentence.

3.01   God thought _____ .

          _____ families were important

          _____ families were not important

          _____ there should be no families

3.02   When someone goes away _____ .

          _____ you cannot communicate

          _____ you forget him

          _____ you can communicate by phone or letters

3.03   Most jobs _____ .

          _____ use communication

          _____ use no talking

          _____ are all alike

3.04   Some words begin with a g that sounds like _____ .

          _____ k

          _____ s

          _____ j

3.05   A person who can talk two languages and helps people understand each other is a _____ .

          _____ teacher

          _____ translator

          _____ doctor

Write yes **if the sentence is true. Write** no **if the sentence is not true.**

3.06 _____ Parchment is made from animal skins.

3.07 _____ The first paper was made of cloth.

3.08 _____ Countries need to communicate with each other.

3.09 _____ Alexander G. Bell invented the wireless.

3.010 _____ One famous satellite is named Telstar.

3.011 _____ Without communication it is very hard to have a happy family.

3.012 _____ You should never tell your parents how you feel.

3.013 _____ New ways of communication have made new jobs.

3.014 _____ Leaders of countries cannot communicate if they do not have the same language.

3.015 _____ Communication can help countries work together.

EACH ANSWER, 1 POINT

$\frac{12}{15}$

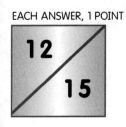  Teacher Check _____

Initial   Date

 My Score

page 33 (thirty-three)

IV. COMMUNICATION WITHOUT SOUNDS

Although talking is easy for most people, people can communicate without sound. People have all sorts of ways of making themselves understood. This section will help you think of other ways to communicate.

WORDS TO STUDY

diary	(di a ry)	A daily record of events.
expression	(ex pres sion)	A look on a face showing the feelings of the person.
mime		Using only movements to express a story.

Ask your teacher to say these words with you.

Teacher Check _____

Initial   Date

HANDS AND FACE

Moving your hands or face are a form of communication. When children in a classroom raise their hands, the teacher understands that they have a question to ask or know an answer.

People clap their hands when they are pleased. They raise them in greeting or wave them in farewell. People bow their heads to show respect and point to things to show interest.

Expressions of the face can tell a lot about people, too. Smiles and frowns tell how happy or sad they are. When people are reading, their faces are still and usually rather sad. As soon as someone else is near, though, whether talking or not, people will show interest or boredom or pleasure or some feeling by changes in the expression of their faces.

Babies communicate very well before they know how to talk. They learn to hug and kiss their family when they are pleased. They pull a hand when they want someone to come and look at a toy. They will hit a teddy bear or kick a truck to show anger. Moving hands or showing expressions on their faces are ways to communicate.

Most children enjoy clowns. Clowns are funny because they have odd, often sad, expressions painted on their faces, and then do funny things. Many clowns are quite silent during their acts. They pull up pretend chairs and sit on them, or paper pretend

Clown

walls. They are miming. **Mime** is using only movements to tell a story. You can try using mime on the playground.

Write the answer using words from the LIFEPAC.

4.1   People _____ when they are happy.

4.2   Babies learn to communicate _____ they know how to talk.

4.3   Movements and _____ of the face are a way to communicate.

4.4   Clowns use funny faces and _____ to make people laugh.

4.5   When babies are very pleased, they might give someone a _____ .

LETTERS AND DIARIES

Writing as a way of communication has already been talked about in this LIFEPAC. Letters and **diaries** are special ways of communicating that are different from books and newspapers. Letters are special because they mean extra time and thought have been spent in telling something.

Using a phone to thank a grandmother for a birthday present is easy and is a nice thing to do. If a letter is written, then grandmother has it to read again and again. She knows that writing the letter was a special job, so she is especially pleased.

Do this activity.

4.6   Write a letter to a family member or a friend. Make the letter at least three sentences long. Write the letter at home and bring it to class for the teacher to check what you have done. Then mail it.

Teacher Check _____
                    Initial   Date

How to Write a letter

Diaries are thoughts or things that happen during the day written down just for the writer to see. Putting ideas and thoughts onto paper often makes them easier to understand. Writing down what has happened during the day gives a record of events that helps people to remember. A ship's captain keeps a "log," a written report of everything that has taken place that day.

He writes about the weather, where the ship is, and any special happenings on the ship. He writes in his log every day.

Two famous explorers, Lewis and Clark, kept diaries of their adventures. They explored the northwest lands of the United States. They wrote about the hard things they had to do, the adventures with wild animals, the help from Indian tribes. They also told about rivers and mountain ranges they saw. These diaries helped the explorers to remember their months of travel. They make exciting reading today, as well.

Write yes **if the sentence is true. Write** no **if the sentence is not true.**

4.7 _____ Letters are a way of communicating.

4.8 _____ Diaries are often just for the writer.

4.9 _____ Writing about happenings on a ship is called "times."

4.10 _____ Writing often needs more thought than talking.

4.11 _____ Explorers never write anything down.

SIGNS

Every day people use signs as a way of communication. The signs do not even have to have words on them to be understood. Driving down the road and seeing a ⊗ or a STOP should show a railroad crossing and a stop to everyone. Outside a barber shop you will sometimes see a red and white pole. Long ago this red and white pole was a sign for someone who would fix up cuts and hurts like a doctor. Now it means that a barber is inside. On some of the freeways across the country there are signs like ⛽ and 🍽 that show you where you can get off the next exit and buy gas and food.

Deaf people communicate without sounds. They use their fingers and hands to make signs. Some of the signs are letters of the alphabet, others mean whole words or ideas. This sign language is called ASL, American Sign Language. People use it all over the world. In many countries, news is given with someone using the sign language as well as someone talking. Now deaf people can "hear" the news, too.

See the ASL alphabet!

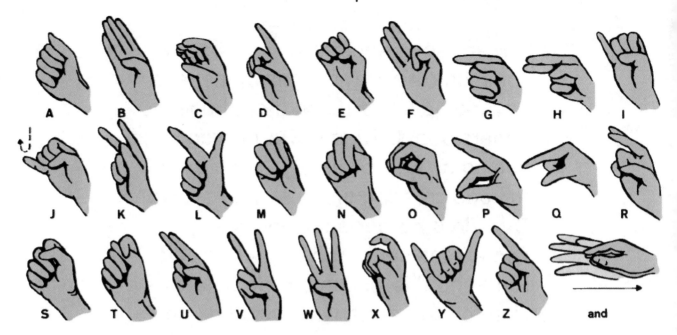

Do these activities.

4.12   In sign language this word is _____ .

4.13

 In any language this sign means

_____ .

4.14   If a picture of a boot hung outside a shop, what sort of

shop would it be? _____

4.15   Are signs a way of communication? _____

4.16   Road signs are very important. Draw one you see
        often.

Review
REVIEW
Review
Study what you have read and done for this last
Self Test. This Self Test will check what you
remember in your studies of all parts in this
LIFEPAC. The last Self Test will tell you what parts of
the LIFEPAC you need to study again.

SELF TEST 4

**Write the numbers to tell what happened first, second,
third, and fourth.**

Communication in Bible times

4.01 ____ papyrus

4.02 ____ parchment

4.03 ____ stone tablets

4.04 ____ paper

Communication in modern times

4.05 ____ telegraph

4.06 ____ television

4.07 ____ phone

4.08 ____ computers

Write the answer from the list on the line.

expression computer sign

scroll   diary   translator

4.09 Writing on papyrus that is rolled up is a

_____ .

4.010 A _____ is a machine that stores

words and thoughts.

4.011 People who speak different languages use a

_____ to help them

communicate with each other.

4.012 People write what they have done or thought of each

day into a _____ .

4.013 A person shows whether he is sad or happy by the

_____ on his face.

4.014 News can be shown using _____

language as well as talking.

Put an (x) in front of each true statement.

4.015 _____ We talk to God today by phone.

4.016 _____ God talks to us in the Bible.

4.017 _____ We learn to talk in school.

4.018 _____ People communicate in many ways.

4.019 _____ Most letters travel by horse today.

4.020 _____ ASL is a sign language for deaf people.

4.021 _____ The STOP sign tells you to eat.
4.022 _____ One way to spell the long /ē/ sound is EA.

EACH ANSWER, 1 POINT

18 / 22

Teacher Check _____
Initial   Date   My Score

Review
REVIEW Review

Before taking the LIFEPAC Test, you should do these self checks.

1. Did you do good work on your last Self Test?

2. Did you study again those parts of the LIFEPAC you did not remember?
   Check one: ☐ Yes (good)
                 ☐ No (ask your teacher)

3. Do you know all the new words in "Words to Study"?
   Check one: ☐ Yes (good)
                 ☐ No (ask your teacher)

NOTES

NOTES

NOTES